ALL YOU NEED IS A PENCIL

THE ← ← " ← ← " ← WEIRD, WACKY, AND UNUSUAL ACTIVITY BOOK

Activities, Games, Doodling Fun, Puzzles, and Much, Much, Much, Much More!

JOE RHATIGAN

ILLUSTRATIONS BY ANTHONY OWSLEY

imagine!

To all my weird fans. —J.R.

An Imagine Book
Published by Charlesbridge
85 Main Street, Watertown, MA 02472
(617) 926-0329
www.charlesbridge.com

ISBN 978-1-62354-077-7
10 9 8 7 6 5 4 3 2 1

WHAT'S THE STRANGEST, SILLIEST, WEIRDEST THING YOU'VE DONE TODAY?

Just pencil your way through the pages of this book and you'll be able to answer this question with confidence! You can tell friends and family that you drew stuff on the bottom of some dude's shoe, solved a spiral crossword puzzle, played the biggest ever game of tic-tac-toe, or even imagined what an alien's X-ray looks like. All you need is a pencil and this book and you'll be planning the next zombie attack, escaping asteroids, imagining animals that don't exist, playing weird telephone, and creating a gross-out alphabet. There are also puzzles to solve, doodles to doodle, and quizzes to answer. So sharpen your pencil and get ready to get your weird on! (No prior weirdness required.)

WHAT'S IN A NAME?

Write down your full name. How many words can you make up with the letters in it?

_____

(Your full name—first, middle, and last)

List the words you come up with here:

1. _____

2. _____

3. _____

4. _____

5. _____

6. _____

7. _____

8. _____

9. _____

10. _____

11. _____

12. _____

13. _____

14. _____

15. _____

16. _____

17. _____

18. _____

19. _____

20. _____

Turn this into a competition with a friend.

_____

(Your friend's full name—first, middle, and last)

List the words your friend comes up with here:

1. _____
2. _____
3. _____
4. _____
5. _____
6. _____
7. _____
8. _____
9. _____
10. _____

11. _____
12. _____
13. _____
14. _____
15. _____
16. _____
17. _____
18. _____
19. _____
20. _____

STEPPED IN IT

This guy just stepped in something. Then he stepped in something else. Finally, he stepped in yet something else. What did he step in? Draw the three items he stepped in on the sidewalk below. Then draw what the bottom of his shoe looks like now.

MINI CROSSWORDS

These bite-size nugget crosswords are great for when you only have a few minutes (or if you have little patience!). The only thing is, you have to figure out which boxes the answers of the clues belong to. **Answers on page 140.**

Things in Your Nose

Clues

One of your digits

Green and slimy, also known as snot

Also on your head

Microscopic stuff that makes you sick

Useful Information:
Your nose and sinuses make about a quart of snot every day!

Monsters in the Movies

Clues

Hairy guy, likes to howl at the moon

Big guy, likes to climb tall buildings

Lizard guy with fiery breath

Dr. Jekyll's other half

Wants to eat your brains

All he wants is blood

Slimy, Squirmy, Hairy Bugs

Clues

Wiggly, lives in the ground

Baby fly

Has eight legs

Looks like it has a hundred legs

Likes to visit the kitchen

This tiny critter sucks your blood

Your Smelly Body

Clues

What you exhale

What drips from you when you exercise

Also known as toots

You put them in stinky shoes

You need deodorant for these

What you gotta do when you gotta go

Outer Space Visitors

Clues

Unidentified Flying Object, for short

Unidentified Flying Object pilot

A space visitor from the movies who wants to "phone home"

A superhero from the planet Krypton

Planet where we used to think most space visitors came from

Things That Could Kill You

Clues

Goes with thunder

Bang! Bang!

When two vehicles crash

Zap!

Shakes things up

Also called a twister

Where chestnuts roast

What happens if you can't swim

Choo-choo

BODY PARTS

These body parts need bodies, and it's your job to provide them!

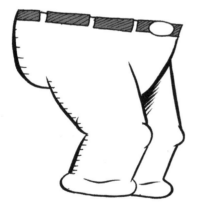

WOULD YOU RATHER: GROSS EDITION

Which of the two unpleasant options would you rather suffer through? Play this gross version of the popular game by yourself or with friends!

Around the Dinner Table

Would you rather...

eat cake with barbecue sauce on top
OR
eat a steak with chocolate sauce on top?

eat ice-cream-flavored poop
OR
eat poop-flavored ice cream?

use mayonnaise made from sweat on your sandwich
OR
use ketchup made from blood on your hamburger?

drink spoiled milk
OR
eat a piece of moldy bread?

suck on a lollipop that fell in the toilet
OR
eat cat food for lunch?

eat one live slug
OR
keep a handful of live slugs in your pocket for a whole day?

At School

Would you rather . . .

take a nap under the urinals in the boys' bathroom
OR
lick the cafeteria floor?

chew a piece of gum that's been stuck under a desk
OR
chew and swallow a pencil?

stick your finger in a classmate's nose
OR
have a classmate stick his finger up your nose?

have your classroom smell like dirty feet
OR
have your classroom smell like dirty armpits?

have a social studies teacher who constantly picks his nose
OR
have a math teacher who farts once a class?

have a principal with three eyes
OR
get served lunch by a lunch lady with dirty fingernails?

spend one month listening to the same Earth science lecture over and over again
OR
spend two weeks living in the boys' bathroom?

walk the hallways with a pair of underwear on your head
OR
walk the same hallways wearing a pair of underwear over your pants?

Personal Hygiene

Would you rather . . .

never be able to brush your teeth
OR
never be able to take a shower?

not be allowed to wash your hands for two months
OR
not be allowed to wash your hair for two months?

stop cutting your nails for one year
OR
wear the same pair of underwear for one year?

smell like rotten eggs all the time but look fantastic
OR
smell wonderful all the time but look wretched?

not be able to bathe for two months but have clean clothes every day
OR
be able to shower every day but have to wear the same clothing for two months?

use a disgustingly dirty toilet
OR
use a clean toilet bowl with a snake in it?

take a bath full of live worms
OR
take a bath full of dead fish?

All About You

Would you rather . . .

have an extra finger on each hand
OR
have a small tail?

grow hair on your tongue
OR
be able to taste with your hair?

have a spider crawl in your ear while you're sleeping
OR
eat live maggots with your rice?

live in a haunted mansion
OR
live in an unhaunted cardboard box under the freeway?

WEIRD TELEPHONE

This game can be a lot of fun when you have a group of bored people (three or more) hanging around. It's like the game of Telephone, but you use paper.

1. Rip out the opposite page or use scrap paper.

2. The first person writes an absurd sentence—the craziest she can think of.

3. The next person reads the sentence and illustrates it underneath. (Don't worry, accurate drawing is not necessary!) Then he folds the paper so the third person cannot see the sentence, just the drawing.

4. The third person looks at the drawing and writes a sentence that describes what is going on in it. She then folds the paper over so the drawing can't be seen.

5. The fourth person reads the sentence and draws it . . . and so on. Use new paper when you reach the bottom of a page. When you're done, unfold the paper and see how close the final drawing or sentence is to the first one!

DON'T THINK TWICE: THE IN OR OUT EDITION

Answer the questions below as quickly as possible without putting too much thought into them. Time yourself and see how many you get right. Don't write in the book if you want to play with friends. **Answers on page 141.**

Scoring: Divide the number of seconds it took you to take the quiz by the number of questions you got correct. The lower your score, the better. For example, if it took you twenty seconds to get nine questions correctly answered, your score would be 2.2. If it took you twenty-five seconds to get all ten questions right, your score would be 2.5. So, in this case, speed was better than accuracy!

Hint: If you don't know an answer, skip it! Remember, the object of this quiz is not only to get as many correct answers as possible, but also to do it in as little time as possible.

1–3: Awesome!
4–6: Smarty-pants
7 & up: Not bad!

Fill in the blanks: Is it "IN" or "OUT"?

1. Gross me _____!
2. He's part of the _____ crowd.
3. They fell _____ love at first sight.
4. He got chewed _____ by the principal today.
5. That's a drop _____ the bucket.
6. Wow, I'm really _____ of it.
7. He's _____ like Flynn.
8. The ball is _____ your court.
9. I hope to find _____ the truth.
10. Go _____ on a limb.

FINGER-FLICKING GOOD

Get set to play with your pencil in a way you probably haven't before: by flicking it! Put the sharpened tip of your pencil on the page and balance it there with one finger on the eraser end. Then with your other hand, flick the pencil so that it leaves a mark along the paper as it moves. Practice in the space below. Got it? Let's play!

Off to the Pencil Races!

Grab a friend and two pencils for this game. The first player chooses a lane on the next page and places the tip of his pencil on the starting line. Then he flicks the pencil forward, trying to keep it in the lane. If the pencil mark stays within the lane, the player circles where the mark ends and starts there on his next turn. If the mark strays outside the lane, he must go back to the starting line. Then the next player goes and does the same thing in her lane. The players takes turns, starting from where their previous pencil marks ended. Whenever a pencil mark goes out of the lane, you have to go back to your previous mark at the next turn. The first player across the finish line wins!

FINISH

FINISH

START

START

QUOTEWORD PUZZLE

The puzzle grid below contains a quote by author Lauren Myracle. In order to figure out what it says, answer the clues and fill in the grid with the correct letter. Go back and forth between the grid and the clues until you complete the quote! **Answers on page 141.**

1			2	3	4	5		6	7		8	9		10	11	12	
	13	14	15	16	17	18		19	20	21	22	23					
24	25	26		27	28	29		30	31	32	33		34	35	36	37	
	38	39	40	41		42	43		44	45	46	47					

A. His toy truck fell off the table and now it is _____.

__ __ __ __ __ __
24 46 30 38 43 7

B. It's getting late; we'd better _____ now.

__ __ __ __ __
2   47 32 4 45

C. The Declaration of Independence was _____ by Thomas Jefferson.

__ __ __ __ __ __ __
11 21 27 26 15 18 12

D. _____ the Bear says only YOU can prevent forest fires.

— — — — — —
29 42 40 41 36 33

E. No one likes _____ kids at a restaurant or grocery store.

— — — — —
19 35 6 39 37

F. You think you're so smart, but you can't pull the _____ over my eyes.

— — — —
41 10 20 17

G. _____-oh, I think I just deleted my homework by mistake!

— —
25 44

H. What's the _____ of the book you're reading?

— — — — —
34 1 28 13 5

I. The shy boy raised his hand _____.

— — — — — — —
16 3 8 14 23 22 9

SIMPLY A-MAZED

Create your own mazes using the grids on the following pages.
Your friends will be a-mazed when they see the puzzles
you made for them to solve!

Tips

—Don't forget to have one path that leads from start to finish. If you want, lightly draw the correct path before filling in the rest of the maze. Just make sure you can erase the solution completely.
—Create lots of choices for the puzzle solver to make the maze challenging.

START

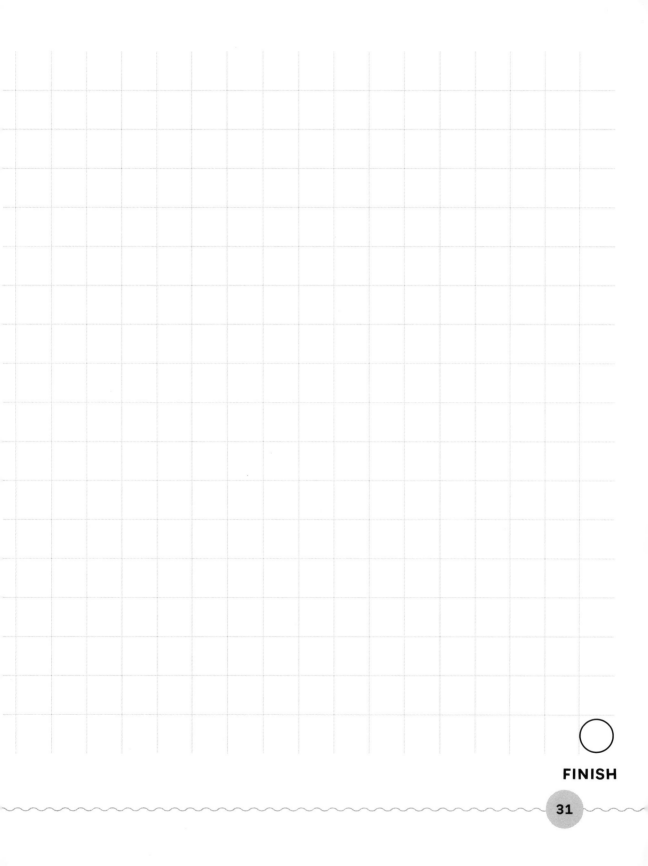

FINISH

Now try creating a maze with no grids. You can incorporate curved pathways now!

HOURS TO GO

Studies show that we spend nearly one-third of our lives sleeping. How do you spend the awake parts of your days? Time yourself from the moment you wake up to the moment you go to sleep and fill out the hours and minutes below:

How many hours did you sleep?

_____

How much time did you use for eating?

_____

How much time did you use for getting dressed?

_____

How much time did you spend looking at yourself in the mirror?

_____

How long did it take getting to and from school?

_____

How much time did you spend talking to friends?

_____

How much time did you spend texting with friends?

_____

How much time did you spend doing homework?

_____

How much time did you spend attending classes?

_____

How much time did you spend watching TV?

_____

How much time did you spend looking at funny cat pictures on the Internet, or doing other things online?

_____

How much time did you spend running or playing a sport?

_____

How much time did you spend at after-school activities?

————

How much time did you spend bathing?

————

Total:

————

(The total should come close to 24 hours!)

What would your perfect day look like? Use this space to write it down hour by hour:

7 A.M.

_____

8 A.M.

_____

9 A.M.

_____

10 A.M.

_____

11 A.M.

_____

12 P.M.

_____

1 P.M.

_____

2 P.M.

_____

3 P.M.

_____

4 P.M.

_____

5 P.M.

_____

6 P.M.

_____

7 P.M.

_____

8 P.M.

_____

9 P.M.

_____

BUILD YOUR OWN SWISS ARMY KNIFE

A Swiss Army knife is a pocketknife with various tools, such as a can opener and a screwdriver. The attachments are all inside the handle of the knife and can be pulled out when needed. Build your own Swiss Army knife below! What kind of wacky things would your knife have inside?

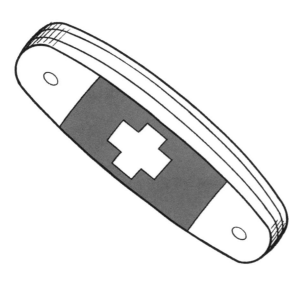

IMAGINARY TEXTS

Do monsters use textspeak? What emoticons would a baby use? Use the boxes to "text" with the people and/or things listed below.

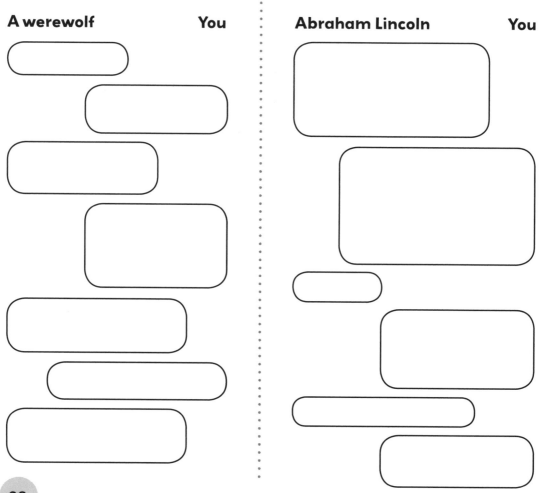

A werewolf   **You**   **Abraham Lincoln**   **You**

Your pet **You**   **Your favorite celebrity** **You**

A baby You **A polar bear** You

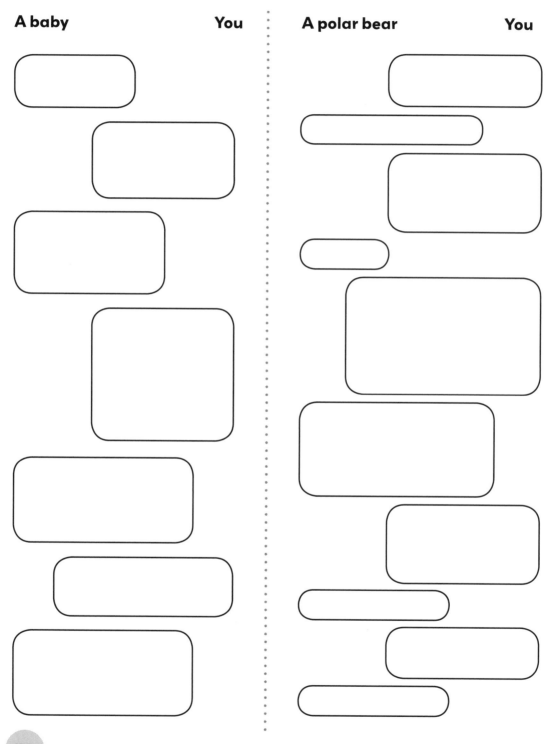

Your school desk   **You**

The germ that made you sick   **You**
last time you fell ill

SILLY WAYS TO WASTE YOUR DAYS

Too much time on your hands? Why spend them wisely doing homework and chores when you can waste them doing one or more of the useless activities below?

1. Play a game of Monopoly (or other favorite board game)... by yourself.

2. Watch television with your eyes closed. Then when that gets boring, open your eyes but turn down the sound.

3. List your ten favorite things in the whole wide world here:

1. _____

2. _____

3. _____

4. _____

5. _____

6. _____

7. _____

8. _____

9. _____

10. _____

4. Redecorate your room.

5. You're locked in your school with no way out. What would you do?

_____

_____

_____

_____

_____

_____

_____

6. You have three wishes. What would you wish for?

  1. _____

  2. _____

  3. _____

7. Memorize a poem or song.

8. Rip out a page of this book and see how many times you can fold it.

9. Balance stuff on different parts of your body.

10. Check the couch cushions for lost change.

11. Practice drinking a cup of water while lying down.

12. Invent a new way to tie shoelaces and convince your friends to try it. Write the instructions here:

_____

_____

_____

_____

_____

_____

13. List your least favorite things in the world here:

_____

_____

_____

_____

_____

_____

14. Do everything in slow motion.

15. Alphabetize your books by the authors' middle names.

16. Practice your signature backward here:

_____

_____

_____

_____

_____

17. Start saying, "You know it!" to anything anyone says and see if it catches on.

18. Write the lyrics to your favorite song here:

_____

_____

_____

_____

_____

19. Give names to all your stuff.

20. Throw playing cards in a hat.

21. Try touching your elbow with your tongue.

22. Write the story of your life in six words:

_____

_____

_____

_____

_____

_____

23. Draw whoever's in the room with you right now.

24. Find all the pencils lying around the house and sharpen them.

25. Create a list of more silly ways to waste your days.

_____

_____

_____

_____

_____

_____

_____

_____

_____

_____

_____

_____

NO CROSSING!

This is a very simple yet time-consuming game. All you need to do is fill as much of these two pages as densely as possible without crossing your pencil marks. Ready? Set? Go!

CONNECT THE PLOT LINES

Look at the two seemingly unrelated images below.
Write a story that connects them.

_____

_____

_____

_____

Now write a story for this pair of images!

_____

_____

_____

_____

_____

_____

_____

_____

_____

WATCH YOUR P'S AND Q'S

The grid below is a giant tic-tac-toe game. Grab a friend and start playing. Decide who will be P and who will be Q and who will go first. Take turns placing your letter in the grid. Here's how the scoring works:

3 letters in a row (across, down, or diagonal) = 3 points
4 letters in a row (across, down, or diagonal) = 10 points
5 letters in a row (across, down, or diagonal) = 20 points
6 letters in a row (across, down, or diagonal) = 40 points

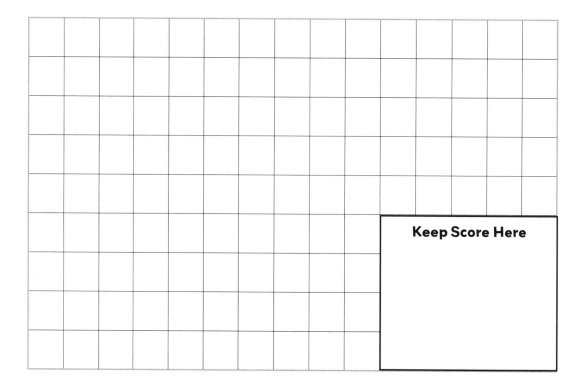

Keep Score Here

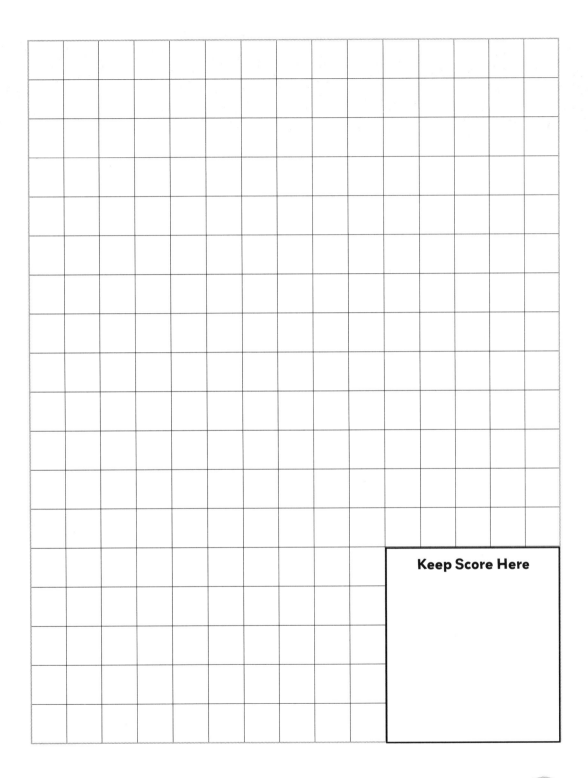

Keep Score Here

THE QUICK BROWN FOX . . .

"The quick brown fox jumped over the lazy dogs" has all the letters of the alphabet in it. This sentence accomplished the feat using only thirty-seven letters. Try coming up with your own sentences containing all twenty-six letters of the alphabet. Can you do it with fewer than thirty-seven letters? Cross out the letters as you go so you know when you've gotten them all!

A   B   C   D   E   F   G   H   I   J   K

L   M   N   O   P   Q   R   S   T   U   V

W   X   Y   Z

WEIRD TRIVIA

You know what would be really weird? If you knew the answers to all these trivia questions. **Answers on page 141.**

1. Which of the following has not been reported to have fallen from the sky?

    A. Cats
    B. Frogs
    C. Snakes
    D. Fish

2. Which is not an ingredient in snot?

    A. Water
    B. Salt
    C. Proteins
    D. Fats

3. The rafflesia flower is known for being what?

    A. The widest flower
    B. The ugliest flower
    C. The stinkiest flower
    D. The most poisonous flower

4. What is pediculosis?

    A. A fear of feet
    B. An infestation of head lice
    C. Athlete's foot
    D. A disease in which you lose your eyebrow hair

5. The largest cockroach is . . .

    A. 3.8 inches in length.
    B. 4.8 inches in length.
    C. 5.8 inches in length.
    D. 6.8 inches in length.

6. Which of the following is not an official record kept by Guinness World Records?

    A. Most alarm clocks smashed using feet in one minute
    B. Most toilet bowl seats broken by the head in one minute
    C. Most live goldfish eaten in one minute
    D. Most ice-cream scoops thrown and caught in one minute

7. Which of these can you do in space?

    A. Burp
    B. Scream
    C. Go to the bathroom
    D. Breathe

8. Which animal was not kept as a pet at the White House?

    A. Miss Beazley, a Scottish terrier
    B. President Kanga, a kangaroo
    C. Emily Spinach, a snake
    D. Nanko, a goat

9. The word Crayola means . . .

    A. oily chalk.
    B. colorful sticks.
    C. rainbow pencils.
    D. wax pencils.

10. Which of the following used to be an Olympic sport?

    A. Dodgeball
    B. Tug-of-war
    C. Kick ball
    D. Running bases

THINGS THAT GO BUMP IN THE NIGHT

At night you hear all sorts of strange noises. Draw what you imagine is out there while you're lying in bed.

Creak!

Bang!

Snap!

Grrrrrr!

Screech!

Hoooooo!

Waaaa!

Clatter!

Groan!

Squeak!

Slither!

CROSSWORD TREE

Two down is a well-known saying. Solve the across clues in the puzzle on pages 66–67 to figure it out while using the other down clues to help. Many of the clues are easy, but there are a few that may stump you! The stars in the boxes indicate spaces between the words of the saying. **Answers on page 142.**

Across

1. Short for "miniature"
3. Camping housing
6. Cheesy pie
7. Pens need it to write
8. What you feel when you stub your toe
9. Where toothpaste is kept
10. What ghosts say
12. How we elect presidents
13. A police officer IDs herself with this
14. What your eyes do with words
15. What boxers do
16. Backed _____ a corner
17. What you do when pushing the door doesn't open it
18. This feeling lives in your heart
20. 3.141592
21. Santa might give you one for Christmas

22. You throw these for bull's-eyes
23. Animal many think is wise
25. What you do to your engine to warm it up
26. Happily _____ after
27. Lionspeak

Down

2. A well-known saying
4. Keeps your head from falling off your body
5. A movie that tells the true story of a person's life
11. You'll find it attached to a pocketbook or backpack
13. Another word for "puke"
17. Overwhelming fears
19. I love you _____ much
24. Opposite of tell the truth
25. "River" in Spanish

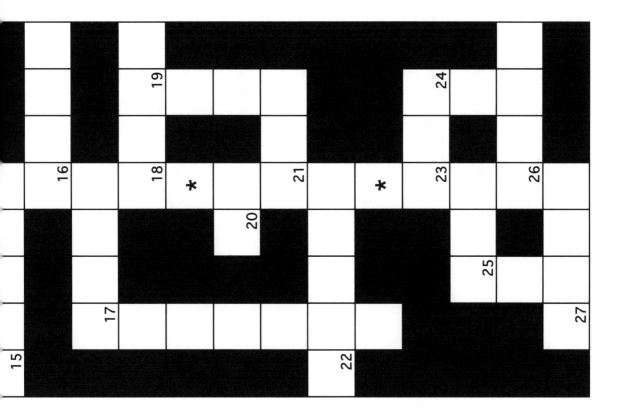

MONSTERS AND ALIENS

These monsters are missing body parts.
It's your job to supply them.

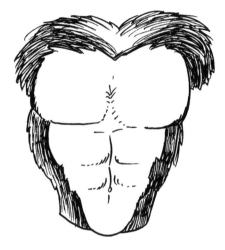

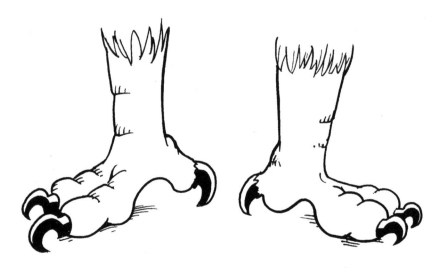

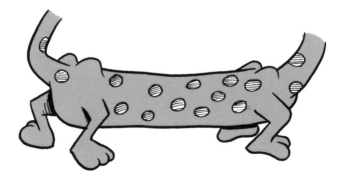

ASTEROID FLICK

By flicking your pencil across the page, see if you can spacewalk safely from the spaceship to the wormhole. If you hit an asteroid, you have to start all over again. Turn to page 24 for instructions on flicking your pencil.

FIVE DOTS

See the sets of five dots on the next page? It's your job to draw a person in each set with one of these dots at the drawing's head, two at his hands, and two at his feet.

Here's an example:

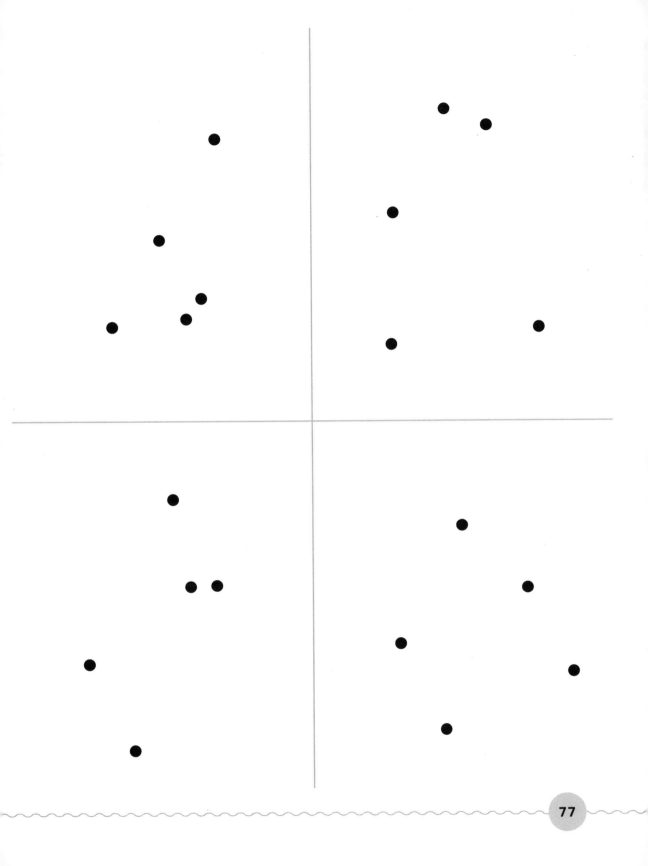

Now, challenge a friend to a game of Five Dots. Use the following blank pages to take turns placing five dots anywhere on the page and have the other person attempt to draw a person!

SPIRAL CROSSWORD

This puzzle may make you a tad dizzy! **Answers on page 143.**

Across

1. A very large and fast digital processor
5. He keeps the birds away from the corn
7. Grown up
9. Concealed
10. A squirrel would like one
12. You wear these on your feet to help you slide down a mountain
13. What plants do when you stop feeding them
14. What one hails to get somewhere quickly
15. Members of the King and Queen's family
19. Mom's mom, to you

Down

1. Sliding down a snowy hill on one wide plank
2. The old man _____ deeply about his dog
3. The number of strokes it normally takes a golfer to get a ball in the hole
4. Having a pet is a big _____
5. A small piece of wood in your finger
6. This bird spends a lot of time banging away on trees
7. They ruin picnics
8. An unproven explanation from a scientist
11. Another way to say "hello"
16. Belonging to oneself
17. That TV cost an _____ and a leg
18. A small child

MAKE YOUR OWN SPIRAL CROSSWORD

Starting at the asterisk, come up with solutions for the crossword puzzle. Once you have words for each spiral clue, see how many three-letter words you can add as extra clues. Draw a box to create the clue. Once you're done, set up the blank grid on the following page for a friend to solve.

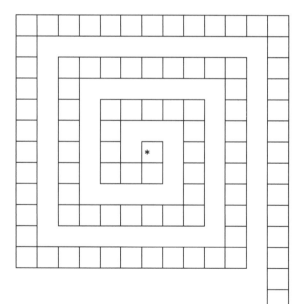

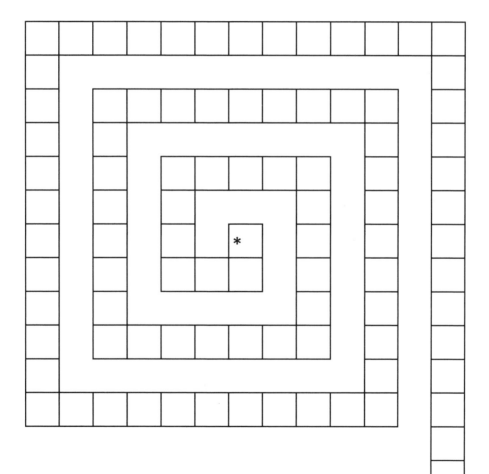

DEAR SCARY MONSTER . . .

Write a letter to something that used to scare you when you were little (the monster under the bed, the neighbor's dog, ghosts, dragons, etc.).

Dear_____,

Now write the scary thing's reply.

Dear _____,

(Your name)

WHAT'S FOR DINNER?

Tired of the same old same old at dinnertime? Spice up the meals below with worms, maggots, guts, eyeballs, and more!

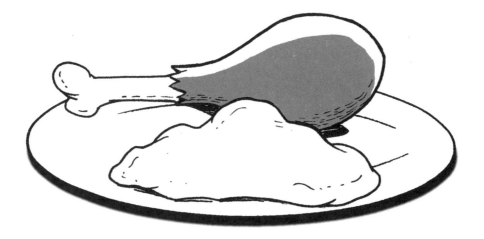

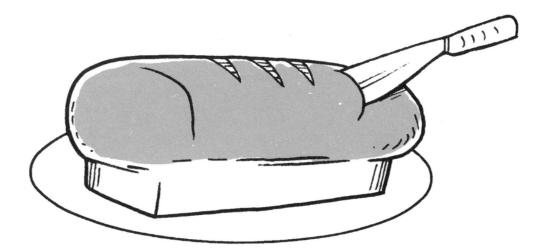

LIST 'EM

How many monsters can you name from movies, books, video games, songs, etc.?

_____

_____

_____

_____

_____

_____

_____

_____

_____

_____

_____

_____

How many can a friend list?

MAP IT

Using only your memory, use the grids to map out your whole school with all the rooms labeled. If you don't want to think about school, try the same thing with your home.

PENCIL FLICK GOLF

Use this spread to create a nine-hole golf course. Draw sand, water, rocks, etc., as if you're looking down at the course. Don't forget the tees and the holes! Then, using the pencil flick method on page 24, tee off and count how many flicks it takes to get to each hole. If you hit water, you have to add a stroke to your flick count, go back to your previous point, and retake your turn. If you hit sand, rocks, or other hazards, only half of the pencil mark counts and you must erase the second half.

ZOMBIE ATTACK!

The zombies are coming, and you need to prepare! One of the best ways to get ready for a big event (whether zombies in your backyard or a backyard barbecue) is to make a few lists. Use the prompts below to help you get organized!

List 1
To stay ahead of the zombies, you'll need to keep moving, so all you can take is one backpack. What would you put in the backpack?

1. _____
2. _____
3. _____
4. _____
5. _____
6. _____
7. _____
8. _____
9. _____
10. _____

List 2
There's safety in numbers, so you need to decide who will go with you. What skills do they have that will help you survive?

1. _____
2. _____
3. _____
4. _____
5. _____

6. _____
7. _____
8. _____
9. _____
10. _____

List 3
What will you use to protect yourself?
You don't only have to use standard weapons!

1. _____
2. _____
3. _____
4. _____
5. _____
6. _____
7. _____
8. _____
9. _____
10. _____

List 4
How will you get food?

1. _____
2. _____
3. _____
4. _____
5. _____
6. _____
7. _____
8. _____
9. _____
10. _____

List 5

You have a couple of weeks before the zombies come. What skills do you think you should brush up on?

1. _____
2. _____
3. _____
4. _____
5. _____
6. _____
7. _____
8. _____
9. _____
10. _____

List 6

In the event you become a zombie, whose brains do you want to eat?

1. _____
2. _____
3. _____
4. _____
5. _____
6. _____
7. _____
8. _____
9. _____
10. _____

MUTANT IMAGINATION

Draw what you think these animals would look like:

Koalaphant
(Koala + Elephant)

Killer whaleguin
(Killer Whale + Penguin)

Turtleraffe
(Turtle + Giraffe)

Kangacat
(Kangaroo + Cat)

Hamstape
(Hamster + Ape)

Crocobird
(Crocodile + Bird)

Raccorse
(Raccoon + Horse)

Pudgehog
(Pug + Hedgehog)

Duger
(Duck + Tiger)

Snooster
(Snake + Rooster)

**Cowbit
(Cow + Rabbit)**

**Pigapus
(Pig + Octopus)**

WOULD YOU RATHER: WEIRD FOOD EDITION

These are real foods from around the world. Which of the two would you rather eat? Just remember that even if it's gross to you, somebody somewhere is enjoying it!

. . . .

Would you rather eat . . .

. . . .

Stargazey Pie (a Cornish pie featuring eggs and potatoes with fish heads sticking out of it)
OR
Casu Marzu (sheep's milk cheese fermented by maggots—from Sardinia, Italy, and illegal everywhere)

Beondegi (steamed or boiled silkworm pupae, from Korea)
OR
Obara (a Slovenian stew made from dormice)

Chapulines (Mexican grasshoppers)
OR
Fugu (raw pufferfish, which if you're not careful will kill you)

Bird's Nest Soup (the name says it all—made in China)
OR
Head Cheese (a Scottish meat jelly made with the head of a calf or pig)

Balut (duck embryo boiled alive in its egg, common in Southeast Asia)
OR
Kopi Luwak (an African style of coffee from beans that have been eaten and pooped out by civets, which are small nocturnal mammals)

Sanguinaccio Dolce (an Italian pudding made from chocolate and the blood of a freshly slaughtered pig)
OR
P'tcha (jellied calves' feet from Eastern Europe)

Jellied Moose Nose (an Alaskan dish of sliced moose snout)
OR
A-ping (fried tarantulas from Cambodia)

Smalahove (a Norwegian dish made from smoked sheep's head)
OR
Escamole (ant larvae from the roots of agave or mescal plants, from Mexico)

Sannakji (a raw Korean dish consisting of live octopuses with sesame and sesame oil)
OR
Khash (a sort of stew made from cow's feet, head, and stomach, popular in South Asia and Southeastern Europe)

Blodplatter (Swedish blood pancakes made of pork blood, milk, rye flour, dark molasses, onion, and butter)
OR
Chahuis (edible beetles from Mexico)

WEIRD ALPHABET

Think of something sticky, slimy, oozing, scary, weird, or otherwise abnormal for each letter of the alphabet. Can you draw them all, too?

A

E

B

F

C

G

D

H

I

N

J

O

K

P

L

Q

M

R

S

W

T

X

U

Y

V

Z

CHANGE ONE LETTER

Here's a game for people who like to play around with their words. You can play by yourself or with up to four players.

The Object
Be the last player to be able to make a new word

What You Need
2 pencils

What You Do
1. Choose someone to go first. This player picks a four-letter word and writes it down on the first line below.
2. The next player changes one letter of the word to create a new word.
3. The first player (or third, depending on how many people are playing) then has to change one letter of the new word to create a third word. This player cannot use the previous word.
4. Play continues until someone cannot come up with a new word.

For example:
Player one: stop
Player two: slop
Player one: slip
Player two: slim
Player one: slit
Player two: flit
Player one: flat
Player two: flap

X-RAY VISIONARY

We put a bunch of interesting people and things behind
an X-ray machine. What do you think we found?

TIC-TAC-D'OH!

This is a simple game you can play by yourself. All you have to do is fill in the tic-tac-toe grids with letters so that you spell out words across and down.

Like this:

B	E	G
A	R	E
H	A	T

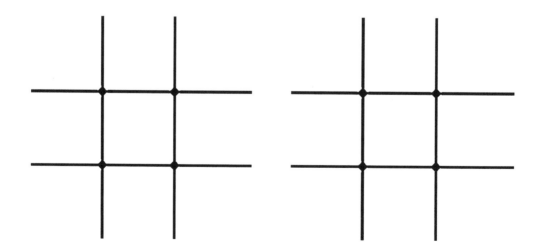

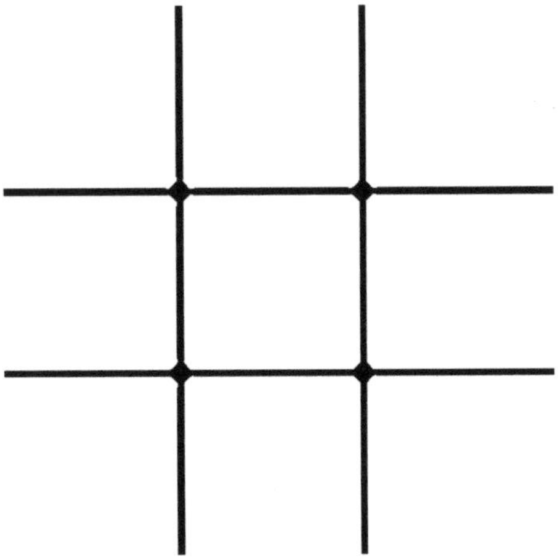
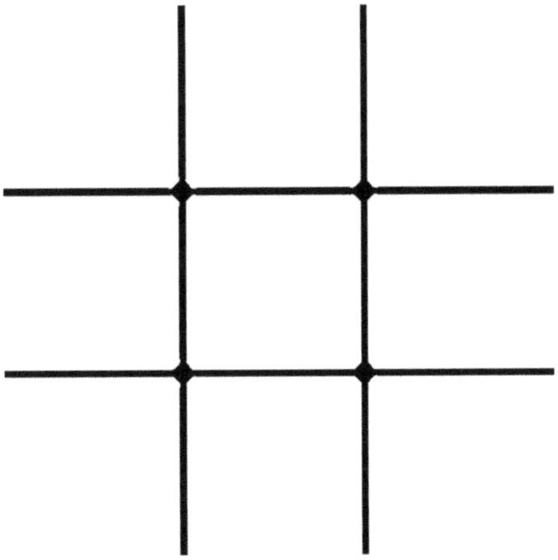
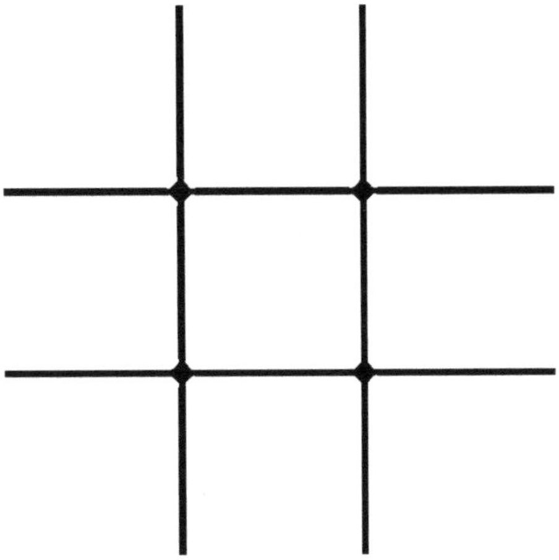
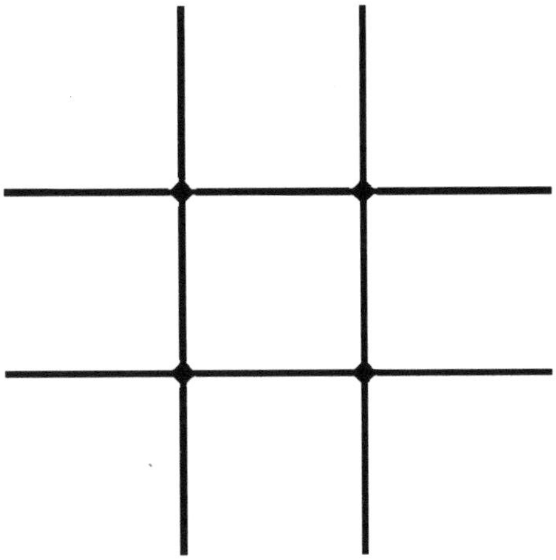
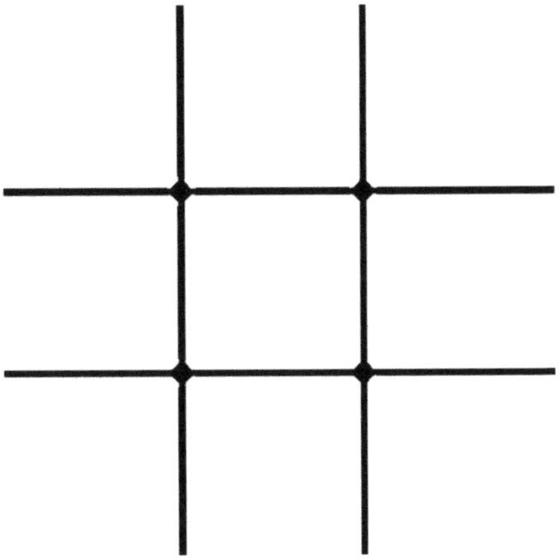
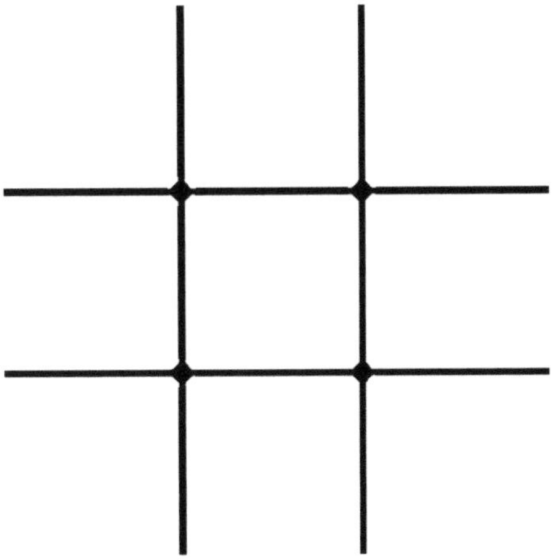

BUILD YOUR OWN CELL PHONE

Here is a normal cell phone. Boring, right!? How would you jazz it up? Also, what apps would you want on your home screen?

HURT BURT

Grab a friend to play this game. See poor Burt in the middle of these pages? Player one's job is to draw something that will hurt Burt (poison arrows, wild dogs, etc.). Player two's job is to save Burt from harm (with shields, armor, etc.). Keep taking turns attacking or protecting Burt until there's no more room on these pages to draw anything!

FACE IT

These heads are in the middle of experiencing something.
Draw the expression you think best fits each sentence.

The cat brought in a live mouse.

Spent five hours finishing a homework assignment.

Saw a ghost.

**Someone scratched his
fingernails across a blackboard.**

Found $100 on
the sidewalk.

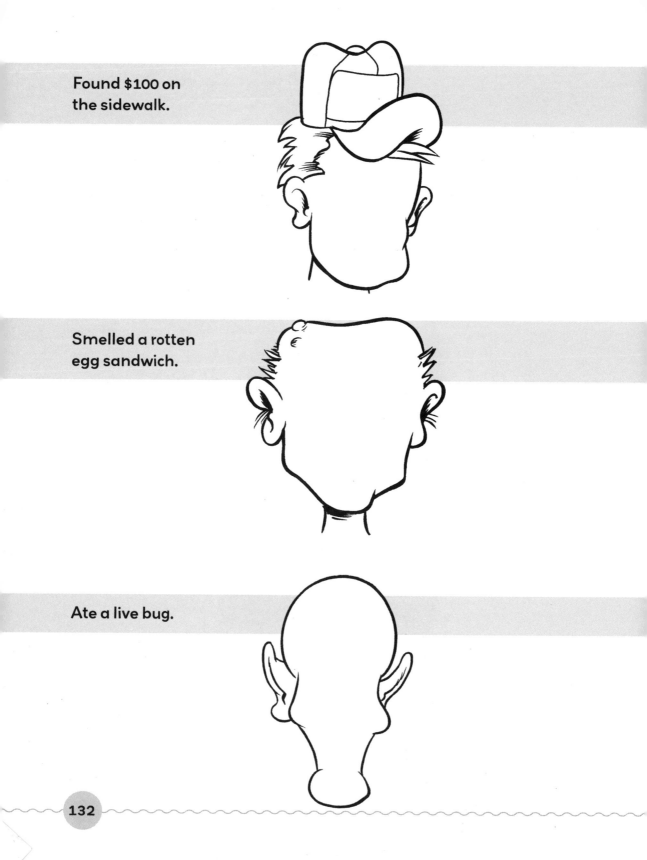

Smelled a rotten
egg sandwich.

Ate a live bug.

Found a finger
in his French fries.

Failed her social studies test.

There are zombies
on the back lawn!

DON'T THINK TWICE: THE IDIOMS EDITION

Answer the questions below as quickly as possible without putting too much thought into them. Time yourself and see how many you get right. Don't write in the book if you want to play with friends. **Answers on page 143.**

Scoring: Divide the number of seconds it took you to take the quiz by the number of questions you got correct. The lower your score, the better. For example, if it took you twenty seconds to get nine questions correctly answered, your score would be 2.2. If it took you twenty-five seconds to get all ten questions right, your score would be 2.5. So, in this case, speed was better than accuracy!

Hint: If you don't know an answer, skip it! Remember, the object of this quiz is not only to get as many correct answers as possible, but also to do it in as little time as possible.

1–3: Awesome!
4–6: Smarty-pants
7 & up: Not bad!

An idiom is a phrase that has a meaning that's different from its literal meaning. For instance, "The ball is in your court" doesn't mean there's a ball in your court, but instead that it's up to you to take the next step. Finish these idiomatic expressions:

1. Don't count your chickens _____.

2. Don't look a gift horse _____.

3. Don't put all your eggs _____.

4. Don't bite the hand _____.

5. Don't rock the _____.

6. Don't cry over spilled _____.

7. Don't give up your _____.

8. Don't hold your _____.

9. Don't judge a book by _____.

10. Don't throw bricks when you _____.

GERMS EVERYWHERE

Here are a few germs you can draw on the following items. Don't forget to wash your hands!

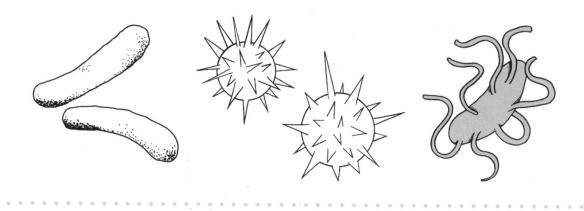

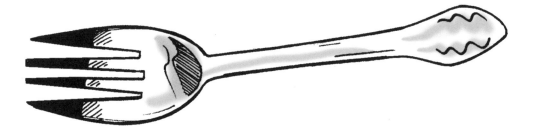

Mini Crosswords (page 8)

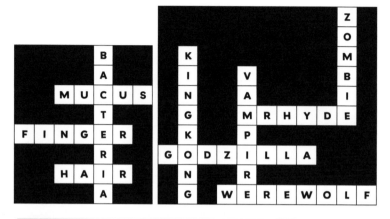

Don't Think Twice: The In or Out Edition (page 23)
1. out; 2. in, 3. in; 4. out; 5. in; 6. out; 7. in; 8. in; 9. out; 10. out

Quoteword Puzzle (page 26)
A. broken; B. leave; C. written; D. Smokey; E. whiny; F. wool; G. Uh;
H. title; I. timidly

I live in my own little world, but it's okay. They know me here.

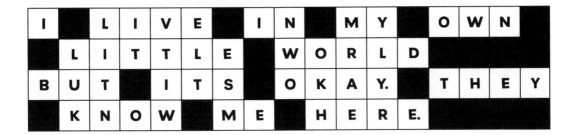

Weird Trivia (page 57)
1. A: Rain of flightless creatures has been reported throughout history; however, no one has ever seen it raining cats *or* dogs.
2. D: Mucus (snot) is produced by your body to protect your lungs from bacteria, viruses, dust, pollen, and more.
3. C: Known as the corpse flower, it smells like rotting meat to attract insects that fertilize it. It grows in the rain forests of southeast Asia.
4. B: Lice have been feeding on humans for at least ten thousand years.
5. A: The *Megaloblatta longipennis* is a winged cockroach found in Peru, Ecuador, and Panama. It can have a wingspan up to eight inches.
6. C: Guinness World Records discourages dangerous stunts and stunts that harm animals or others.
7. C: As long as you're using a zero-gravity toilet.
8. B: Miss Beazley lived in the Bush White House, Emily Spinach lived in Teddy Roosevelt's White House, and Nanko lived in Abe Lincoln's White House. An alligator once lived in a White House bathtub, but there has never been a kangaroo in the White House.

9. A. The name of the most famous crayons combines the French word *craie*, which means *chalk*, and *ola*, which is short for *oily*.

10. B. Tug-of-war was an Olympic event between 1900 and 1920.

Crossword Tree (page 65)

Spiral Crossword (page 83)

S	U	P	E	R	C	O	M	P	U	T	E	R
N				A			A					E
O		S	C	A	R	E	C	R	O	W		S
W		P		E					O			P
B		L		A	D	U	L	T		O		O
O		I		N				H	I	D		N
A		N	U	T		H		E		P		S
R		T		S	K	I		O		E		I
D	I	E					R		C	A	B
I		R	O	Y	A	L	T	Y	K		I
N		W		R		O			E		L
G	R	A	N	D	M	O	T	H	E	R	I
										T
										Y

Don't Think Twice: The Idioms Edition (page 135)

1. before they hatch; 2. in the mouth; 3. in one basket; 4. that feeds you;
5. boat; 6. milk; 7. day job; 8. breath; 9. its cover; 10. live in a glass house

OOH, A BLANK PAGE? THINK OF SOMETHING WEIRD TO DO WITH IT!